LITTLE WHALE

words&pictures

© 2023 Quarto Publishing Group USA Inc.
Text © 2023 Anna Brett
Illustrations © 2023 Carmen Saldaña

First published in 2023 by words & pictures,
an imprint of The Quarto Group.
100 Cummings Center,
Suite 265D Beverly,
MA 01915, USA.
T (978) 282-9590 F (978) 283-2742
www.quarto.com

Assistant Editor: Alice Hobbs
Designer: Clare Barber
Art Director: Susi Martin
Publisher: Holly Willsher

A CIP record for this book is available from the Library of Congress.

ISBN: 978-0-7112-8355-8

9 8 7 6 5 4 3 2 1

Manufactured in Guangdong, China TT042023

LITTLE WHALE

illustrated by
CARMEN SALDAÑA

ANNA BRETT

SPLASH!

Hello, I'm Little Whale, a humpback whale. Dive into the ocean and join me in my watery world for some fun.

This is my mom, dad, and the rest of my pod. That's the name for our family group.

4

My cousin and I are
only four months old,
so we are called calves.

5

The ocean is our home.
We have so much space to
explore, and we love to swim
and swim and swim!

We like both cool and warm water and
spend time in both temperatures.

But we are currently on an
adventure to find the cold waters
of the Antarctic Ocean where
there's plenty of food for us.

7

We only swim together as a pod when we are traveling. My mom leads the way through the water, Dad swims alongside me, and we have my older brother, aunt, and cousin with us as well.

We are named humpback whales because we have humps on our backs, in front of the dorsal fin.

We are gentle giants and enjoy swimming
alongside friendly dolphins or interacting
with seals from time to time.

9

We all have dark gray, waterproof skin with white on the underside of our tummies, fins, and tails.

My fins work like powerful paddles to help propel me through the water and my tail helps me steer.

Our heads are knobbly. These bumps help with our senses and are called tubercles.

Small creatures called barnacles like to attach themselves to us as well. Look how many Dad has on him!

We don't breathe
through our
mouths like other
mammals. We have
a blowhole.

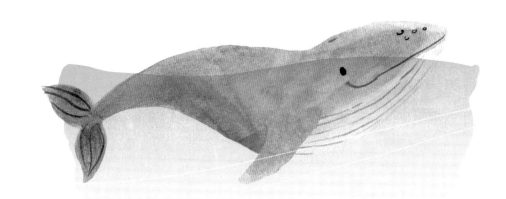

This hole on the top
of the head is where we
breathe in air before
diving under the water.

We can stay
under for up to
30 minutes.

Then, when we resurface,
we exhale through here
as well, creating a spray
of mist.

I love being underwater, but it's so exciting when Mom says we can play on the surface! Breaching is like jumping for us—I swim quickly up to the surface, and then using my powerful tail I lift my body and leap out of the water, splashing back in on my back.

My brother enjoys leaping
out and then splashing
back in on his side!

15

Until our journey to the Antarctic Ocean began, we were in warm tropical waters.

16

This is where my mom and my aunt chose to give birth to me and my cousin, in a sheltered inlet.

We return to this tropical spot at the same time every year, some years to breed, and then the following year to give birth.

I am spending my first few months of life drinking Mom's milk to give me lots of strength for our big swim.

I swim directly underneath her to suck up the thick milk she releases. It helps me build up blubber—a layer of fat under my skin that will keep me warm when we reach the cold water.

The long journey between our warm water vacation and cold water home is called migration. Although the tropical waters are safe and fun for us, the food we survive on is found in the Antarctic Ocean thousands of miles away.

We don't eat much during the migration swim. We live off stored energy in our fatty blubber reserves.

21

Mom and Dad's diet consists of small fish, krill, and more krill! They gulp up these tasty little shrimp in their thousands by swimming through a shoal with their mouths wide open.

We have plates called baleen in our mouths instead of teeth. They act like a strainer to filter the krill from the water and into our mouths.

My brother touches my flipper
to tell me that Dad has
spotted some more food.

There aren't many krill
in this area so it's important
for the adults to catch as many
as possible, to build up energy
during our big migration swim.

Mom, Dad, and my aunt blow bubbles out of their blowholes while circling the krill in a spiral shape to create a net of bubbles. This groups them together in one place, so they are easier to catch... then it's feeding time!

Seagulls circle above, hoping to catch any leftovers.

We are huge creatures, but we still need to be aware of predators in the ocean.

Orcas and great white sharks can hurt us if
they choose to attack. Mom swims directly below me
to keep an eye out for predators rising from the deep.

27

If we do sense danger, we can warn others in the pod by using our tails to slap the water.

The more force we use, the greater the danger as we try to ward off an attack.

I also like slapping my fins on the surface of the water. It's a handy way of communicating with my family.

Listen! Dad is singing! He makes a series of moans, howls, and cries to create a unique song that he sometimes continues for hours.

The sound travels for large distances and can be used to attract females or to mark territory. I can't sing like him yet, but I can make a few noises and clicks.

Thank you for joining me for the day!
As the sun is setting, it's now time for
us to have a short nap.

We only sleep for 30 minutes at a time. That's because we need to surface regularly to breathe, and also keep our bodies moving so we don't get too chilly.

But there's still time to take a few more big breaths and put on a show before we rest. Enjoy this rainbow spray and think of me every time you look out at the ocean. Goodnight, everyone!

FACTS AND PHOTOS

It was so fun to have you swim with me and my family today, thank you for joining us. Read on for some more interesting facts about us humpback whales.

Here's a reminder of all the interesting things about us whales!

Mother and calf humpback whales resting in a shallow reef

- There are around 84,000 humpback whales found in oceans all around the world.

- They can migrate up to 5,000 miles every year, swimming between their warm breeding waters and cold feeding grounds.

- Their name comes from the small hump in front of the dorsal fin.

- Male humpback whales' songs can be heard up to 19 miles away.

- Humpbacks belong to a group of species called baleen whales, which also includes blue whales and minke whales.

Humpback whales surfacing to reveal their humps

Humpback whale tail splashing out of the water

FACT FILE

Average length: 56 feet (females are usually larger than males)

Average weight: 40 tons

Lifespan: Up to 80 years old

Diet: They eat up to 1.5 tons of food a day (mostly krill)

TIME TO DIVE

As the sun sets, Mom whale is slapping her tail to tell Little Whale it's time to dive underwater. Which of these shadows matches her tail?

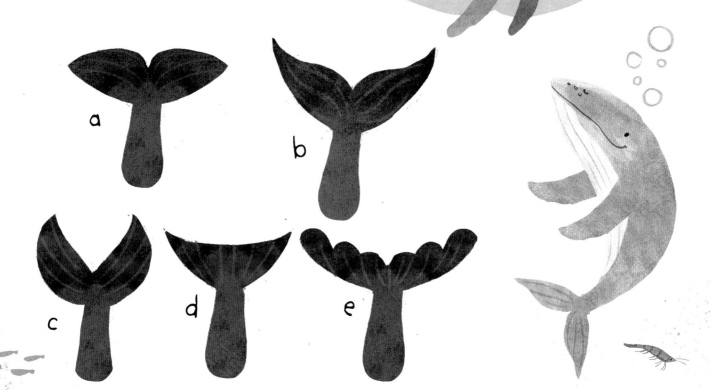

a

b

c

d

e

Whales love to breach on the surface before diving down deep. Can you figure out which jigsaw piece completes the picture?

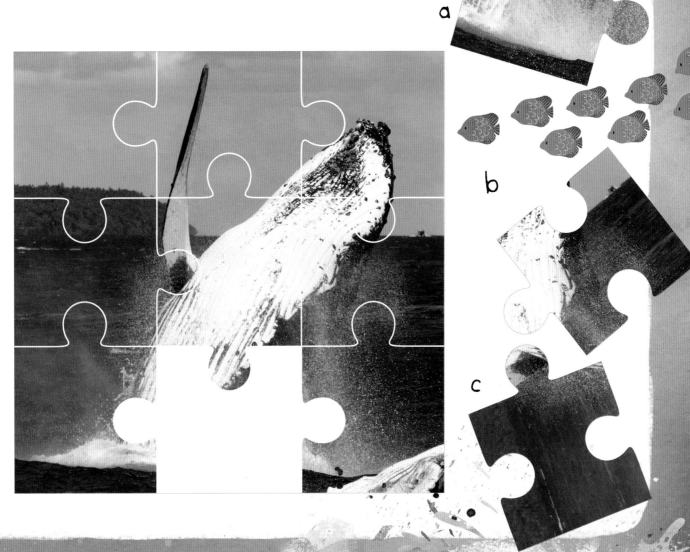

CONSERVATION AND WHALE WATCHING

Thankfully, humpback whales are not listed as an endangered species. There are plenty of them in the sea. But this hasn't always been the case.

In the 1900s they were hunted almost to the point of extinction, which means there would have been none left at all. Luckily whaling is banned today.

It is important to care for all animals and banning hunting is a major step. But climate change and pollution may also affect the whales found in our oceans.

Tour boat watching humpback whales off the coast of Ecuador

If the water temperatures warm up around the world, then there will be a reduction in the number of cold water habitats for krill, which is the primary food source for humpback whales.

Humpback whale feeding on anchovies in front of a boat of whale watchers in California

Humpback whale fin surfacing in front of small tour boat

Whale watching boat trips are a great way for marine biologists and the general public to safely observe whales. Tours also help educate people about these beautiful marine mammals and reinforce the need to protect our oceans. This is only if boats always keep their distance, and don't interfere with the whales or pollute the water around them though.

BIG AND SMALL

Mom and dad whales look very similar, and they are both huge! But if you have a closer look, you should be able to spot five differences between these two.

Which line of teeny tiny krill should Little Whale follow to reach the swarm at the end? How many krill can you count in this line?

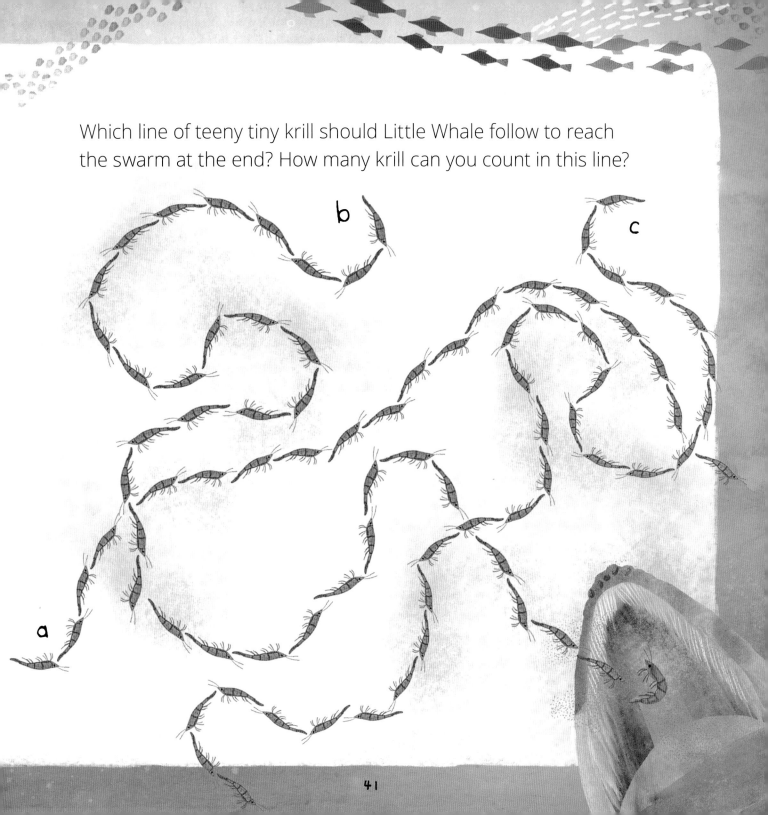

b

c

a

MAKE AN EGGCUP WHALE

YOU WILL NEED

- Empty egg carton
- Coloring pens or paint (the color you'd like your whale to be!)
- Scissors
- Blue pipe cleaner
- Black felt-tip pen
- Sheet of white paper
- Glue

1 Begin by cutting out one of the cups from your egg carton. Ask an adult to help you if you need.

2 Color or paint the cup in your chosen whale color.

3 Using the scissors very carefully, snip or poke a hole into the top of the eggcup.

4 Next, take the pipe cleaner and cut it in half. Then fold each half in half and twist the two pieces together at the base.

5 Poke the pipe cleaner through the hole in the eggcup, and then fold over each of the four ends to create little arches. This is your whale's spray.

6 Now it's time to add your whale's face. Draw on two eyes and a smile using your black pen.

7 Color in your sheet of paper whatever color you'd like your whale's tail and flippers to be. Then cut out one tail shape and two flipper shapes, as shown here.

8 Fold the straight end of the tail, add glue, and stick it inside the eggcup. Then glue and stick the two flippers onto the sides of the eggcup.

WELL DONE, YOUR WHALE IS COMPLETE!

NOW YOU COULD MAKE A WHOLE POD!

MEET MIGALOO!

There's one very special humpback whale that can be found swimming in the waters off Australia. His name is Migaloo and he's completely white!

Migaloo's tail surfacing

Model Migaloo floats over the 2018 Commonwealth Games opening ceremony

Humpback whales are usually always gray with white undersides, but like humans they can be born with a condition called albinism. This means they lack color pigmentation in their skin. Migaloo is an albino whale and he's become famous because of it.

First spotted in 1991, in waters off Byron Bay, Australia, he's been seen migrating up and down the coast most years since. His song has been recorded and various photographs have been taken of him, but a law has been passed that prevents boats getting within 1,640 feet of him. This is so he remains protected and can hopefully continue to live a long and healthy life.

Migaloo was given his name by the elders of the local aboriginal community in Hervey Bay, Australia. The word means "white fella." They believe that albino animals should be respected because they are extra special.

Migaloo spotted off Byron Bay in Australia

I would love to bump into Migaloo out in the ocean! Hopefully I will one day.

QUIZ

After all these hours by the water, why not test your knowledge of the amazing humpback whale? See how many of these questions you can get right.

1. Is a group of whales called a swarm or a pod?

2. Humpback whales can only survive in warm tropical waters. True or false?

3. What do whales most like to eat?

4. What is it called when whales leap out of the water and splash back in?

The answers are on page 48.

8. What is the long journey whales travel on each year called?

9. Whales can blow bubbles to create nets in the water to catch krill. True or false?

10. Do males or females sing songs?

5. Humpback whales sleep for 8 hours overnight. True or false?

6. What are young whales called?

7. The blowhole is used by the whale to:
a) Breathe air in and out
b) Eat
c) Go to the toilet